The Told World

Also by Angela Gardner

Thing&Unthing Vagabond Press, Sydney 2014
interference (chapbook) Ampersand Duck 2014
Of Sky (chapbook) Ampersand Duck 2012
Views of the Hudson Shearsman Books 2009
The Twelve Labours with Gwenn Tasker, light-trap press 2009
The Night Ladder, with Lisa Pullen, light-trap press 2009
Parts of Speech University of Queensland Press 2007

Angela Gardner

The Told World

Shearsman Books

First published in the United Kingdom in 2014 by
Shearsman Books
50 Westons Hill Drive
Emersons Green
BRISTOL
BS16 7DF

Shearsman Books Ltd Registered Office
30–31 St. James Place, Mangotsfield, Bristol BS16 9JB
(this address not for correspondence)

www.shearsman.com

ISBN 978-1-84861-371-3

Contents

for

Laurie Duggan and Rosemary Hunter
Ian Friend and Robyn Daw

History Painting

It's the sense of emptiness
wind in long grass
square kilometres of levelling irony.

Out here in the grand scale
what price heroic death, in brushmarks
that indicate parachuting angels.

Across this alien windswept plain
as foreground intersects midground
sporadic housing makes way

for other figures carefully rendered.
While children are legging it away
into the picture plane, our sense

of past exhausting their every step;
until at the vanishing point, human
must give way to gods.

Add processional detail: a throat
of rocks, balancing acrobatics of gold
painted in small movements,

finally receding in saccades below
the clouds. Is it there now in your mind's
eye, the telling space of it almost grasped?

The painted body slumped while the mind
sings historic events. Yet it never was, this
vitrine of finger-pointing inside this frame.

The terrible choices you've considered
in witnessing the retreating figures fly
from death upon the almost naked plain

will disappear as easily as the plain itself
appeared before your eyes. Until
it is itself

no more than the usual neurons' trick
of light.

METAMORPHOSES

Metamorphoses

I

Street after street held back in unanimity
drowned in brick and tile containment
flat suburbs of white bread television stupor
droning and drowsing out to the rivermouth.

That paradoxical question from philosophy:
How to live?

Above, the sky is radiant with risk
turning shadows, luminous glances, break
throughs in motion, charge and discharge.

II

And if I was

without echo, the mirror in my skull falling
away — dimensions swallowed
sensation voiceless, stilled, diminishing.

The broken suitcase, the ladder,
a whole neighbourhood quieted
night forcing its way down nerve paths
to the eyes, full, lithe.

III

On the driveway of my own house
looking forward rather than back —

the car locked in its carport
lighted windows reach out
stars that compete with countless cities

with the spun thread of story.
Step back into the old self, jarring return
riven, expendable
hard to ignore the void
left behind.

Dawn loosens
    — the day careless, brightening.

IV

Mount Coot-tha staked with television masts
a parrot, a flash of colour superimposed.
Pale-headed, its cobalt wings
rearrange to brief respite on a backyard fence
top wire quivering slightly.

The morning air held, like breath, expectant
not even a distant lawnmower.

V

Here,
where the river dawdles along pockets
shifts past the point
then out, out of sight, under the bridge.

You'll come to cliffs
with equipment laid out: ropes, harnesses,
other tackle and instruction
shouted from the rim.

But first you must stand on the river path
searching for footholds in your mind
for a way through
to a vision of self, climbing like morning
impossible, perfect.

VI

The pale-headed parrot balances
lacking the effort required
to lift from entropy

    — gravity reaction sleep, poised on cyclone
wire in the misfires of its boundaries
all pleasures held a moment

VII

Or a map — alive
no different than forgetting
hurt held together by dust,
ashes mingled with spit and blood to carry
in our heads, to navigate the day

The body fails
there is no guarantee of semblance.

Biomechanics conceal rougher modulations
electro-chemical properties of matter
that fail to shape the poetics

Nothing
will alter absolutes
into flight.

VIII

The substance of the earth, the figuration of sky
the realm between

where we believe
all happens

cognate cloudburst
the indivisible self in disarray
as time erodes, disorders, without repair
pivot tipping, trapped by desire
to be of some other clay.

IX

I stare
at unbroken coastline an incoming tide
sea-edge at the moment of imperceptible turn
nothing is settled

Listening now for the wind to elide

instead it picks up. Stencil clouds jostle
within an empty frame. As if the body's interlocutor
is free from its own weight or responsibility
        — until flesh forgets
to pressure surrounding air.

X

None of it need be

A wholeness ghost-limbed or absent
gets caught in the machinery

tongues fail or fade and birds in half-light
fly up
colourful, silent, hardly known.

XI

I risk my body to
a pharmacopoeia of change
blinded certainty that buffets against closure
deaf-mute acquiescence

the mirror searches for reflection
new-made — on water (in others' eyes)

light pools collect under cloud gap
rainfall already passing
the air in motion

XII

A man paddles past on a bicycle
a stream of cars
yellow flash silver flash
words spray paint under bridges

a differential is at work
skin shuttered against itself
a horizon few dare recognise

We take leave of ourselves
then cannot follow

Each of us unfinished will not survive
our own upheavals
our transformations

the rescue trace

of boundaries mapped by others.

I'm capturing pixels

photons as they hit the plane of the lens

an idea that shape-shifts
ever-absent, ceded to, and distracted
by event

— birds make song pathways in air.

THE TOLD WORLD

Landscape With Birdsong

Try to imagine yourself there:
back from danger, exhilarated,
the handsome family you return to, kissing
each in turn.

There is this side of the river and the other
our different selves
—— the one who looks at the mountain
the one who rests in the valley
each an unreliable world
unimaginable to the other.

In the moments that we believe
before theatre begins
some truth is hammering in the cavity of the body.
So needy we hardly recognise our own
in the birdsong.

Nothing can prepare us,
not the discomfort of the sky we rise to meet
nor the leavened thrust of wings
into the cloudworld:
while the heaven of each remains unfinished.

The Sum and Its Parts

Not a rerun of *Star Trek:*
The Next Generation or a reload of *I*
Love Lucy but the day in my head replayed
and the nervous system closed up

— when I got to the burial ground
summer had already come looking in
to the light-filled hole
the child on his rocking horse, distinct
in his world, horn and ears alert.

Did I say this was a love story?
The pressure of new sap faced with love
embodied: vapour-clouded, breathless.

When Actaeon went into the forest
it was full summer, all that tells of the season
said differently through sunshine.

So late in the year. We step through this
curtain, to crouch, where last night's windfall
lies bruised upon the grass

the upturned forest in sad decline, the pity of it,
so meekly arriving, dog-helmeted as you
and I console ourselves.

The problem is not flesh and bone but viscera,
the shining consciousness it maintains
as beauty, hard above the poisoned blood.

The Told World

A day of vision — fields bound by rain,
in unaffected shanties not merely human:
birds moving out to the open.

And what's to be done with the hexbolt
and stop-action, when absent more gently
— isn't it meaningless or not quite truthful?

Compare our three hundred days of sunshine
or morning wordless: your hand, that
operates so delicately in complicit grounds.

It is a period of exile
with its pivotal shot, impartial of shadow,
and light that frames the narrow window,

to stand disproportionate in daylight
and perfect avoidance, the *told-world*,
thin as celluloid, we risk at every step.

A prospect — I lose belief!

While we are apart,
there is comfort in blades of muscle
and bone. How could there not?

Alert to a whole repertoire of touch,
away from all necessary politeness.
So fall the blows, the big ugly voices,

covered only in darkness and singing.
The birds fly back. Somehow they give
no inkling of survival.

The Mathematics of Drift

The air has lifted. Profane however musical
or loud, it leaves no room for our pale bodies
and their translucent desires. Even living

lightly with each other and using whatever
comes to hand can fire out ideas that could
unmake the grammar of the close-up

So even when we leave spaces in ourselves
that allow the body to expel rain and tap water
we collect stones in weighty pocketfuls

to be lost among the broken-down furniture
chipped bowls and lights that refuse to work
as throwaways that oppose this limestone

Mouthing steamy air with something
of text touching a clear afternoon in each other
we walk the uphill streets above the bay

until swum through with tiring conversations
we engage the mathematics of drift. Whole
islands towed out to sea by their rusted piers

toward an absolute of waking intention, untoward
gods of gills, with amphibian lungfuls of air
and the ability to breathe through dampened skin.

Barely Noticeable I

Stencil grass and blow-up
ponies sadly
deflating I stoop

to native violets.
My mind, a mild
and clouded surface.

Women delicately pink
winged and clothed
their silicon flesh parting

under cast iron column arches
garlanded overhead
with pressed metal flowers.

Ticket barriers pulse
in concert, a closed
system in perfect reach

the tool's crude optic
runnelled to paths
dense and chemical.

In the glade's depth
and plasma air's
transmission upward

forty clicks to flagfall
eye pressed to image clutter
trembling without

artful riot of pleasures.
So the body — giving
chase — sidesteps

the complicating forest.

Pastoral

Upon a dark path
a dapple, intermittent flashes
as chemical cascades displace

a rain-filled pit, basement
of an unbuilt highrise,
a water bird guards her nest.

Dog at an updraft
through hexagonal chain-link
of the perimeter fence.

The represented in its net of light
inverted and reversed
travels its pathway beyond the eye.

Barely Noticeable II

The glade's depth
and perspective branching
so am I made

to closed system
perfect reach of the tool's
crude but serviceable optic.

Eye pressed to image clutter
trembling without
the *artful riot* of pleasure and of pain.

Over time in party season
women develop delicate pink wings
and unclothed silicon flesh

that pulses, sidesteps gently
in concert — bread and cherries
barely noticeable —

or stagger drunkenly through
Central Station ticket barriers.
Calls from balconies

sky a blinded window
where I, in the left hand portico,
his wares sucketh.

Up into daylight, upward forty
clicks to flagfall
light years of optic flow

mimesis, the body giving
chase through complicating forests
— miraculous with rain.

Unplanned Centaur

Unplanned centaur you would face
a trick of light
slicing the phloem dappled and ready
on hard vinyl. The canopy erected
just for the hunt, the flooring early,
the women modern non-slip, and day
looking on so decorously. How
beasts channelled by beaters were an act
of kindness none of us can forget.

Turn

eyes adjust. in the intimacy
of mirrors — tippets

fur that laps nakedness
— here you are

a head turns to the soft purchase
of light and beyond

a gesture of love
the darkness we all fade into

Swung Weight / Limit Point

early before the hills

blue skies just cover
modestly by number as

dumb hydraulics climb
the weight of air.

Thunderheads hold

shining fluted openings
lantern guyed

here a single watcher
in fur-lined boots

hauls in.

Milkywhite

i. yes you woke me
— tv and i went to sleep
again
the sky makes a lot of noise
as it breaks
touch-free edges flare
lightning lightening landscape
heat bruising fluod
high in high cloud *for*
we will go musical devices
banks of shale cutting out
the raw stands of trees

if nothing else
graspy milkywhite pressure
of the river's sleeptalk
rust petalled flowers on
their weedy stalks
full cunted open
and rain past five
that calls you back
so close to rupture
quickly or tomorrow
as another self surefoots
these wooded hills

Between

Then after rainfall arrives we wake
to the underside of a wrist or it could be birds
fleeing and the wind stilled of tragedy. The word
between the streaming droplets.
                                                  Bodily,
the sticky resin that solidifies the pockets of air
— the between of it all — but maybe it is just fact
gravitationally confined. We are caught struggling,
words not fully summer, the friar birds singing.

Morning Light

…morning light entering by way of a mouth, you turn

Our bodies: the voices of shadows, unstable but nowhere bright,
as near enough… this long moment changed gorgeously
and now differently costumed. Whole imagined cities
still hover overhead to overlay, in ever-tightening lines,
their well-made feet or walls of reason. Insanity reflected
so that only now it can approach the *condition* of music.
Its materials and architecture wait somewhere singing…
buried in each other's bodies

Here is your opening: pulse, breath

It is Summer
Insects beat their fragile wings against glass
and from the sky, your mouth… cities disappear
and look… it is the unclothed morning light that enters.

The Hindward Air

Sky lit with shifting music
— and the centre elsewhere.

Hands over my eyes
an opening in the hind ward air
dimming our bright scales.

Weep ape
light crashes off water
the birds are filled with heavens.

Cubits or Nanomoles

nothing solid, trepid scarp
of the body

every time you say   I have
songs in my head

the thin air gets fatter,
wetter, heavier

condensing to fig's hard buds
upright winter branches.

when you come home
nothing changes

the sky is water — at the edge
a cliff of clouds.

Another Fall from Grace

All those things I said either side of water and glass
How dark does it get dark? How evening?
While you say — these flowers look like dog penises
their lipstick jack-in-the-pulpit Open mouth gaping

to small perfect teeth of white slipped earthenware
a figure floating against nothing and the crackle-glaze
footprint of clouds across his milky chest. His erect nipples
are birds in a cloudy sky entering sharp and clean.

Scorning even the fragility of bones I translate
from the foreign language of self a person I met once
and have forgotten among the buried mirrors used
to capture the faces of the dead — their mottled skin

fading as our memory has of candle-light and shadow.

Sanctuary

vast — the whole bright
pixilated

banking aircraft

yet under, the tree's dark
green edible leaf

(sward)

we work like birds turning
over the soft fruit — piercing

it is no consolation mother
to sweeten my mouth

your arms are evening
clad the sky undone

Above — the huntsman
passe auant

blunder his gentleman

their dogs to a mechanical hare
always ahead

always coursing
their wide agencies of data

ignorant
of our small tasks

of sanctuary — withheld.

Pollen

Here beneath your skin (beneath mine)
in random openings
is what cannot be said in the slow dying of us.
Waiting takes on a peculiar density
flowers wilt in their vases
while pollen, too late or early for stars
falls in meteor trails.

Bones melt to x-ray clarity
and from dark places, screened and private
we find in their handwritten love poetry
that our pale lines are uncertain
strapped together only by fragments of song
…that will pass (one way or another)

ILIUM

Ilium

after Sidney Nolan's *Gallipoli* Series

I

in the small shallows of midday
he bends to retrieve
fallen colours

slouch hat, bare chest
an emptied beach, flag against nothing
maybe a ship

out beyond the cut-throat rocks

walks the horses back into their shafts,
a ribbon of old picnic race tickets
worn as a shade to his dark face

smoke hazes their position
making the strappers nervous and sweaty
as the horses shift

II

the moment the guns fire
each horse stands
as if backed against bad weather

a range beyond human voice
attempts to hold the sky
to silence

even as it disappears

III

the horse is waterborne — legs kicking
neck a nebulae in Andromeda
exploding shrapnel stars

he surveys the drainage
with its naked dead
the cliffs behind roseate and unhelpful

— it is Ilium unrecognisable

But for the crossfire
the man's languid pose might be love-made
his naked face

untouched

as on a different beach, his lover
before the rain flattened
— or hit his left side

IV

cockade and plume ragged
the grasses on cold white sand
bend over their work

— driftwood in pyres

out there the ships are copping it

all the bright days, the burst
as swimming, they faced each incoming hit
of wave

their touching flesh beset
with exhaustion
bodies ripped in streaming light

— open
washed in blood, adrift
in limp animal-hipped shallows

V

in the act of firing a weapon
he searches for signs of the enemy
for death almost

beautiful

finds his slack arm holding lost shoes
drone and flash in all directions
the sky spilled

VI

into this two-up — unsaddled
the calm young
tread dirty air's comet tail

the pillion flicks aside

one only is capable of moving
faceless, dog-tagged
held crutch and truss
to an armature of metal

they are parts of a gun
oiled to hollow downcast weight
of prosthetic

— weapon equal of the man

VII

in a moment of quiet entering the water
horse and rider are alert
for a trail of bubbles to surface

even here where rock or water belay
to knife point
the sea's uninterrupted search

the world put in its place
distant, voided, cast into water
a horizon lacking solidity

VIII

they are limbed again, jaunted and weightless
no longer stilted to be heel-hauled
from open bodies of water

at play in some otherwhere

and the figure he crosses to
— already falling, gone ahead
dreams emptying like cargo lost at sea

the clean anonymous water
and he the sunlit swimmer
shield arm raised

no longer soldier nor anything from home.

EVERYTHING KEEPS MOVING

Somewhere We Drive Through

Parts of 'the view' torn through
a restlessness of everything carried

not to sleep. Images play outside
in widescreen. Scads of rain

a turn that dead-ends into country
stops for fuel, garage restrooms

while the mind abandons itself
to emotional background

to distance headlong. Eye
diffracts kilometres into daylight

overcomes map omissions against
a horizon laid out like the body.

If not weather then euphoria
starry against glassed screens.

Lines that refuse to meet, our flat
earth geometry, we drive through.

Exit Wounds

Through the shattering glass, crashes now into their lives and
out. All momentum of blood and bone. Furring the dark
its own blind trajectory.

Lies beyond the windshield, the constant video-stream roadway
the singing children strapped in kiddy seats, the polished crystal
screen.

Nothing furred and warm to lift its head from pools of night.
From stop-and-go cross-streets of human traffic.
From the hills unfolding paths.

Nothing breathing in its frame of bone and blood.
Nothing in the dark shapes of trees. Nothing,
not even the night itself.

The family is sealed, towards a dark, only momentarily.
Nothing lies beyond, not the road they drove from
those who wait.

A world folding home. The last town. Now the children
sleep, and the map, alone but for the radio, on low.

How It Works

It travels

with our lives through the dark
yards of broken machinery

birds mid-flight are easing past

a truck on a parallel road
appears static.

Picking up speed
we reach somewhere

only horses on the horizon

we are moving
but we don't notice

and some kind of parallax occurs
out to the margins.

Everything Keeps Moving

Humans send news, with swallows over
the ruins like vectors, plotting something
by their interstices
one civilization to another:

height relative to surface. You know relativity
is rough work, when to walk so fast
legs become blurry.

We put on our party stuff. The weather is cool
partly clouded, no-one will notice the eaves
are dropping.

The sky takes on that grey it uses
when weather sets in: easy on the eyes
like a rain-sheeted grid
and a non-colour so easy on a mind
that says:

stay vigilant to temptation.

Animal Light

Being small and neatly branched
your glanced-at limbs manufacture a pressure:
Oh shiny thing as you rearrange your hair
make me happy.

Mid-deal, water-tower in the background
a suburban species of sleet to the fore,
neither of us makes headway. There is a lot
to misunderstand:

our common creeping from the cost and strut
of machines to
our poorly developed momentum requiring
constant clinical resolve.

Where would we be without GPS?
Imperceptible slowness, manifest
in bemused muscle and patent hand signals.
The truth or perfect.

If I want to hold something nailed down
why strap on a jet-pack?
The air around me is a movie soundtrack
of unopened parachute silk.

Habitat

Until the carried thing itself recognizes, blooms an opened door
and soft, the howling mouth, half-seen remnant
all limbs leap clothed and naked — all manner of measuring
DNA reworked to darkened stripes, captive, still pacing
sun and shadow.
                                        And you, disappearing: a hand, a tail,
the pieces almost joining, pelt rubbed against the viewing windows
and through them a glimpse — a blank shape, an enclosing

as if something put upon, *material*: lump transitions gravity
and the affected flesh how she folds it, holds it, until emptied.

Or Further Still

through skycam or skin we so carefully
unzip — the body below wrecked

beaten mesh of veins and sinews,
its meat (a delicate contagion

nerves buzzing) stripped
from their housing, uninsulated

Pull back its covering: the damage
the body unmade

pull back its covering: beauty itself
taut against the half-life rendering

pull back further still, that anything lasts
the loss of intensity

the gills and you, another self
movement and flux looking back at me.

In Double Mirrors

In double mirrors

true and false

we are frangible

skin’s visible default

bony anchors

loosening ligaments

How negligibly begun

the moment of meiosis

but no less purposeful

zygotes, chiasmic.

In the pull back

sometimes kn\ife

sometimes wound

a vestigial memory

shoulders

of clay

of wax and feathers

lipped

strange and hoarse

into true and false.

Wholeness

no less synonym

no less lip-service

her bright head

as slow doors open

deliver

too milky a creature

and sensation newly

deep or shallow

for an idea of gender.

Or corpus

skin's plasticity

as it clings

ill-fitting

finished

but unfinished.

Leaves us

pliable permeable open

reconstructing

from pauses.

Truth and Falsehood

despite

the phenomenal world all to shadows
inadequate poetics, air and falling
frequencies, a dull rotary whirr righted
on the retina

the cries of other creatures.

We Are Called

Otherwise volatile substance, walks past
and how nearly we are human,
failing and uncontained, the small rain.

What to call our genetic distance?
The unwieldy zorse, the liger, the wholphin,
sometimes jaunty above their smiles.

Centuries the nervous
system transmits of spurious instructions
slights and channels, fraught and sniping

all dismissed with careful knife-work.
What will call them: blind-sight, money
well spent. How uncomfortably close

they come, their carefully constructed surfaces.
Mirrors like our children,
we call them, what shall they call us?

Shapely and Whole

Leave your name that starts shapely
and tricked, whole in a mouth
to a pindrop, spat out less polished
as it loses gloss and spit.

Tricked, hidden in a mouth
(always moderation) the winsome girls
less precious, as they lose gloss with spit.
Their dumbshow comfort persuades us

(always), fighter jets. And they
relive rather than relieve night's terror
Stuff not worth the carry
The future degrades to a shimmer

small sounds
that are lies, still we may choose just one:
loose among the tower blocks.
Too late to retract, wary of the blade,

and if they are all lies, we choose one
its hardened metal rushes us.
Too late we are wary
never mind…

it rushes. Us, back to our bodies
to a pindrop, spat out seemingly,
never mind its loss…
your name starts shapely.

Telephony

New analytics are at work — a difficulty
— processing language with just enough swingspace between
the electronic harness and interactive voice. It's bright sunlight
and you're talking to a machine, and its gateways and repeating
are autistic not deaf! Of course! And it answers back, lost
in the deep of its data, a long voyage that will sing us all
to Paradise.

Breezes, brightly coloured birds, the
lost innocence we crave, regular and scheduled. Remote mice
in harness pull us every which way, straight-eyed to avoid sight
of themselves, the disappointments of where we look
and cannot find, and that incoherence buried just packet deep.

Processes Til Unknown

networked devices lip-synch
all lethal and bio-available
while playback users of euphoria
and chromo step up to play

in the mouse-over, things get
a little chaotic: disparate scaffolds
biological targeting
the inherent chemical arms race

subjects may backtrack instability
to concurrent neural stuff
belief, disbelief… the non-linear
disguised as temporal perception

but splice it any which way
or to any compressed timespace
and it's just gone and gapped
from the biological array

sure it processes til unknown
after the mouse-over
but like I said, and go figure on this:
gapped from the biological array.

A Taxidermist's Natural History

Animals will circle his suburban home
like school children released to clatter
of hooves down stairs, for stealthy paws
to follow. Willing, waiting while we sleep,

the start of their migration taut and silent
against night packs of plastic wrapped dogs
herds of plastic wrapped antelope
himself for safety held behind

his heavy heart. Beneath the crackling power
lines he locks eggshells in drawers, as beetles
heave from pins, birds flap from perches, my
brother knows their stillness.

Glassy eyed dulled feathers, lifeless fur make
the children shriek. Cages and tree-felling
trap these animals. In death in life, behind
closed doors there is nothing to say

we are on this side of glass not talking,
in his realm of minor public officialdom.

Burden

Compare with just, with wing:
the unravel, the very place
the door you lean against
in the usual hardwearing.

The unravel, the very place
with claws, with fletch
in the usual hardwearing
self. You were

with claws, with fletch
with desire. Not ceded
the self you were
phasing (to continence.

Desire not ceded
or) the hunt, its flights
(to continence or to veto
the ordinary beautiful.

Or abdication). The hunt
a different mirror then.
The ordinary, beautiful
to the mirror in the motel.

A different mirror then:
the practice of concealment.
To the bathroom mirror
against appearance.

Against concealment
against the dispossessive
against appearance
…how disembodied we are.

Dispossessive (in fragments)
compare with sky..
…how disembodied we are
in the quiet mirror.

The flimsy bathroom door.
Compare with sky,
and in that quiet mirror
compare with just, with wing.

Featherweight

The shadow of a bird flew past —
a brief darkening.

I thought you had
and then I wasn't sure

…for every reason
the oxygenated blood's welling

bright and asymmetric
a feather, a sonic of sunlight.

The weight of a soul
the weight of a feather

lifted from this shared atlas
this cage of branches,

in opened space that sometimes
I see clearly through.

Altogether too responsive
the sky bare against the body

unable to write even the shadow
of a bird against air.

SOLO ESTOY MIRANDO

Half-Light

I'll start you painting flat. Objects next:
modelling three dimensions until light-gleam
appears on something. Garment folds, soft
dark of velvet, a feather in an angel's wing.
Distance then to frame — landscape
a mirror — so real birds dash against it.
Face and hands last, unless you count
everything pulled from background by light
and darkness   a stillness as it develops.

Solo Estoy Mirando (I'm Only Looking)

Prado, Madrid

green under-paints flesh
the body of the king
jaspe oro y esmaltes
jewelled and blindfolded
assailed by light and milk
the taxi driver philosopher

It is *la adoración de los mages.*
At breakfast a procession of cleaners push trolleys
of disinfectant and cleaning cloths.

*

The sculpture of a penitent polychrome,
wrapped in basket weave
like a mannequin waiting for the January Sales,
while outside every window screams ¡Rabajos!

*

A long gallery of Murillo
a whole deck of holy cards… and look
they have the entire set!

*

Saint Eufemia's *sticky* end
alluded to

…consider the saw blade.

*

A musical angel comforts a nameless saint
— the non-musical and tone-deaf
need not apply.

*

The Virgin reads — the very moment before
the ray penetrates.
Gabriel looks mildly pleased.

*

Behold the blazing ego of The Donor
before Christ's lifeless torso,
the congealed blood around his feet.

*

The audio guide hasn't caught up
with the London loans
it spins details of paintings

to the emptied walls.

*

Dürer — tell the Truth!
Through a window the Bavarian Alps
are picture postcard perfect.

*

Bacchus triumphs over three happy drunks
— for him alone a hermaphrodite squirms
breast cock and bum

(Maria de Hungary get thee to a nunnery).

*

Outside the sex shop on *Calle de la Montera*
a Madrid matron is overcome with laughter
Solo estoy mirando (…it is what we all say).

*

In the gallery too I am only looking
clothed or unclothed, luminous and frontal
the doll (…I hope it is a doll).

*

Danaë and Venus lie beside each other
(different paintings)
…loose-limbed and creamy.

So passive, so distracted
anything can happen:
showers of gold, unfinished music…

*

Double-winged cherub heads fly
unaware of their deformity.
They could sell lottery tickets outside
at home among the limbless beggars.

*

From Velázquez
we learn that clouds part for nobility
...the King looks down upon the Poor.

*

A respectful crowd gathers for *Las Meninas*
Velázquez pauses
to look at us, before he paints again.

*

Goya intervenes:
terror looms, compresses, destroys
leaves so little room for sky,
¡muertas muertas muertas!

...even the hens are dead

*

Against this Poussin appears half— hearted

...a monkey tugs his scarf...

Landscape, we almost say
...isn't that some kind of background?

Brightness

A soft gleam (briefly)
just below the ridgeline.

In trees, wind picks up
manifests a differential movement.

Cause and effect kicking
in every direction
trammelled and indifferent

fearful laughter
(but only for a moment).
Into this, rain splinters along
lost

tracks that prise open silence.
A thousand mutable notes
left hanging

different heights or depths
of transparency
for insects to traverse
in small increments of green.

Our maps for this are strange
and empty
resistant to any aggregate of history

space only a space if filled
conventions of perspective
held in defiance
                                        of distance and detail.

Even so the sky
                                        rests weightless
against a painted overhang of cloud
rearranging slabs of argument into
essay.

Air is as nothing

— it is birdsong starts sunlight
exhalation of new growth, red crown
on blue eucalypt

each silence only a silence
a reprieve
sweet lemons or bitter honey.

Birdsong occupies the garden
settles against dark shadow

and constantly we forget

        — how burns the grevillea
within its bright cargo of honey-eaters.

Night

Holes develop in words
down to the isolated *I*

gesture is background static and
now is a month light as bird bones.

In the narrow streets
out of focus star maps shine

against building walls
blurring and resolving strangely

as festive colanders illegally lit
by street-side cable feeds.

Interference overwhelms
the wall dissolves

night under our feet
the light beyond us.

In the subtle mathematics
of curved spaces

happiness tremulous and salient
is meaningless

the stars fall, the sky.

When I Leave the Clouds

through a window sky
opens   gets lost   closes
unravels fitful gusts of cinema
or nothingness

infinity always escapes this radar
this attempt to order the celestial
and when I leave the clouds
the stars look very cold about the sky

Beyond the Footlights

Dream a darkness beyond the footlights
and even if you cannot stand
to read our eyes for applause or censure
at least we are here

shuffling and shifting as time opens out
into the not yet
and at eye-level we are wrapt in the words
that are your and our only clothing

Meaning both seen and unseen
brushes against our crowding mouths
jostling for an opening, for the wounded beauty
and the cruelty of entry

Joining the Dots

They move furniture
place chairs against walls,
move books unread onto tables.

Disrupted from sky, plough stars
dot-to-dot intersecting space junk,
none of which I see.

Then at intervals, unseen figures
shift it all back and light the lamps
to indicate time has passed.

While I stand in a pool of sky
silent and attentive again
to change what things mean.

How did it get this late?
A lawn, some outdoor furniture

a pale green Banksia flower
swings above monochrome grass.

Look at the ruin of the sky
the stars unable to comfort us.

The Cool Shade

Those commemorative avenues, an equation,
one life for another

how upright are the trees of an emptied country
town in Summer

the browned land falls to dust, occasional clouds:
water towers vapourising in the heat.

Into the hot burden of a day: squabble of birds
sticky residue of flower and fruit-fall.

I drive into and out of each town through arcades
of light and darkness

Those long dry avenues of sun and shade,
sun and shade. Sun

and shade.

Notes

The epigraph is taken from *The Demands of Art,* Max Raphael, translated by Norbert Guterman, Routledge & Kegan Paul, London, 1968. p196

'Sanctuary' "Above — the huntsman/*passe auant*" is an inscription on the margins of the *Mappa Mundi* in Hereford Cathedral. For further information see *Mappa Mundi: The Hereford World Map*, P.D.A. Harvey, Hereford Cathedral 2010.

'Morning Light': the partial quotation "the *condition* of music" (my italics) comes from an essay by Walter Pater on 'The School of Giorgione' (*Fortnightly Review*, 1877).

'Metamorphoses' and 'In Double Mirrors' were commissioned by Johanna Featherstone of *The Red Room Company* for their Clubs & Societies project (2011).

Solo Estoy Mirando was written during a visit to Madrid to the Museo del Prado. The phrase: *jaspe oro y esmaltes* (jasper, gold and emeralds) being an inscription to a display in the Dauphin's Treasure Vault.

'When I Leave the Clouds': The last line is quoted from a letter by Keats. The poem was first published by *Jacket*, then as part of a text/image public art collaboration with artist Ian Friend on the Queensland University of Technology Kelvin Grove Screen (a 50x9-metre billboard beside an arterial road in inner-city Brisbane) September 2009 to April 2010.

'Night' was written for my sister; the lines in italics are quoted from Bei Dao 'Night', though the order is rearranged.

'The Cool Shade' was written as part of the University of Queensland Art Museum/School of History, Philosophy, Religion and Classics residency 'Conflict in History'.

Acknowledgements

My thanks to the editors of the following publications in which these poems appeared, sometimes in slightly different form:

Ampersand Duck 'Swung Weight' (letterpress poetry broadsheet); 'Cubits or Nanomoles' (in the chapbook *Of Sky*); *Arc/Cordite* (Canada/Australia) 'Telephony'; *Australian Poetry Journal*, 2013; 'Ilium (after Sidney Nolan's Gallipoli Series)'; *Best Australian Poems 2010,* Ed. Robert Adamson, Black Inc.: 'Morning Light'; *Best Australian Poems 2011*, Ed. John Tranter, Black Inc.: 'The Sum and Its Parts'; *Colloquy*: 'Landscape With Birdsong', 'Brightness'; *Cordite* 36: *Electronica*, Ed. Jill Jones: 'Animal Light' and 'We Are Called'; *Cordite* 43: *Masque*, Ed. Ann Vickery. 'Barely Noticeable'; *51 Australian Poets*: 'The Told World', 'Sanctuary'; *foame*: 'The Taxi Driver Philosopher', now published as the epigraph to 'Solo Estoy Mirando'; *GreatWorks*:' 'Beyond The Footlights', 'Joining the Dots'; *The Hankie Project*, 'Featherweight' first published as an Artist Book by light-trap press for an exhibition at Barratt Galleries; *Jacket*: 'When I Leave the Clouds'; *interference*, Ampersand Duck 2014: 'Unplanned Centaur', 'The Hindward Air', 'Half-light', and 'Habitat'; *Jacket2*, *Magma*: History Painting; *Perita Reperta*: 'Burden'; *Poetry Wales*: 'Night'; QUT artscreen: 'When I Leave The Clouds' (Public Art project with ArtBunker); *Refashioning Myth: Poetic Transformations and Metamorphoses*, Eds. Jessica L. Wilkinson, Eric Parisot and David McInnis, Cambridge Scholars Press: 'A Taxidermist's Natural History'; *Shearsman*: 'Morning Light', 'Another Fall From Grace'; *Sun Herald* 6 Oct 2011 (p7): extract 'street after street held back in unanimity' from 'Metamorphoses'; *Stylus*: 'Pollen'.

Thanks to the Australia Council for a residency at The Tyrone Guthrie Centre in Ireland, in 2009, where some of these poems were written.

Thanks to The University of Queensland Art Museum/School of History, Philosophy, Religion and Classics for a residency in 2014 as part of the AHA conference 'Conflict in History'.

Thanks to Johanna Featherstone and The Red Room Company who commissioned poems for their Clubs & Societies project (2011).

Thank you to Laurie Duggan, Cherry Smyth, GC Waldrep, Nancy Campbell, Enda Coyle-Greene, Judy Brown and Kerry Kilner who, at different times, read and commented upon the manuscript or individual poems in progress; and to Caren Florance of *Ampersand Duck* for time and space in her letterpress studio.

Thanks to *Australian Poetry Inc.* and QAG/GOMA (Queensland ArtGallery/ Gallery of Modern Art) for their 'Cafe Poet Residency' in 2013 during which 'Unplanned Centaur' was written.

www.ingramcontent.com/pod-product-compliance
Ingram Content Group UK Ltd.
Pitfield, Milton Keynes, MK11 3LW, UK
UKHW041845190726
13854UKWH00002B/723

9 781848 613713